Jake's (

Written by Nicola Romaine

Illustrated by Lesley Danson

RISING ★ STARS

It was a dull day. Mum had been in meetings all morning, and Jake was fed up.

"When can we play a game?" Jake asked.
"Can you get the crayons out, Jake?"
said Mum.

Jake scowled.

"Can I play with my skates?" he asked.

"No, not right now," said Mum.

It's not fair!

Jake got the whisk.
"Can I bake a cake?" he asked.
"No, it's not safe. You need my help,"
Mum whispered.

"Make a game! You like Snakes and Ladders," said Mum.
She gave Jake some card and the little tray of crayons.

Jake cut out some snake and ladder shapes. He stuck them onto the card.

He made the snakes green. Then he added some red scales. Jake got on with the game as Mum chatted.

Jake looked at some elephants in his fact book. He cut out an elephant shape to stick onto the game.

Jake cut out some card in the shape of an ape. He gave the ape a bunch of grapes.

Jake cut out a silver dolphin and a black whale. He stuck one near the elephant and one next to the ape.

Jake looked at his alphabet chart.
He cut out the letters he needed to spell
'Jake's Game'.

Jake just had the start box and the finish box to go. The game was all set!

Mum came to see Jake.
"Did you make all of this?" asked Mum.
"It's the coolest game I have ever seen!"

Jake gave Mum a grin. "Will you stay and play?"
"Yes!" said Mum. "This will be the best part of my day!"

Talk about the story

Answer the questions:

1 Why did Mum tell Jake he couldn't bake a cake?

2 What colours did Jake make the dolphin and the whale?

3 What was the name of the game Jake made?

4 Why do you think Mum said playing the game would be the best part of her day?

5 Have you ever played Snakes and Ladders? Can you explain the rules?

6 How do you have fun on a dull day?

Can you retell the story in your own words?